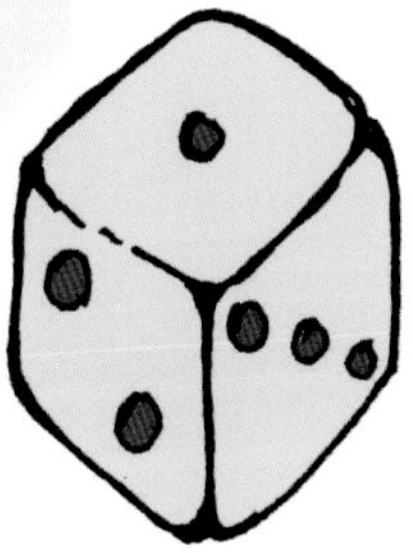

games handbook

INDOOR GAMES!

Lisa Regan

QEB Publishing

Editor: Sarah Eason
Designer: Calcium
Illustrators: Owen Rimington and Emma DeBanks

Published in the United States by
QEB Publishing, Inc.
3 Wrigley, Suite A
Irvine, CA 92618

www.qed-publishing.co.uk

Library of Congress Cataloging-in-Publication Data

Regan, Lisa, 1971-
Indoor games / Lisa Regan.
p. cm. -- (QEB games handbook)
ISBN 978-1-59566-931-5 (library binding)
1. Indoor games--Juvenile literature. I. Title.
GV1229.R44 2011
793--dc22
2010014139

ISBN 978 1 59566-931-5

Printed in China

CONTENTS

HOW TO USE THIS BOOK

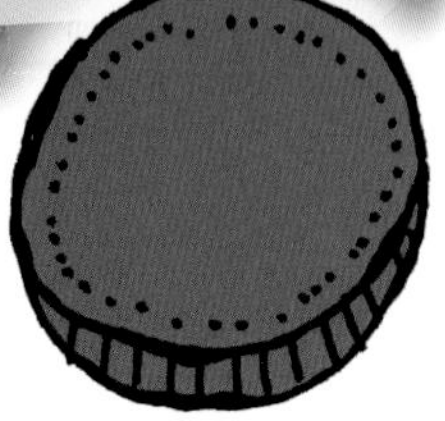

**It's raining, it's pouring,
Being at home is boring!**

What can you do if you are cooped up indoors, you have watched too much TV, finished your book, and played enough computer games? Have no fear—this book is full of games to play inside, without breaking anything or getting on anyone's nerves. You never know—you might end up having so much fun that the grown-ups will want to join in!

You will need

The games are explained really simply, so you can read the instructions and start playing right away. Some of them use everyday items that you can find around the house. You may need to grab a pen and paper to keep score, and a few of the games use dice or a pack of cards. Each game has a list of things you will need at the start, so you can be prepared.

Players

Most of the games are for 2 or more players, to keep anyone who is bored out of mischief. If there is no one to play with you, read the "On your own?" feature to see how to adapt the game and still have fun.

Difficulty

There is a large choice of games to put you to the test, whatever your age or abilities. They are graded throughout the book, from * (very easy) to * * * * * (pretty tricky). Start near the beginning of the book, and challenge yourself as you move on to the harder games at the end.

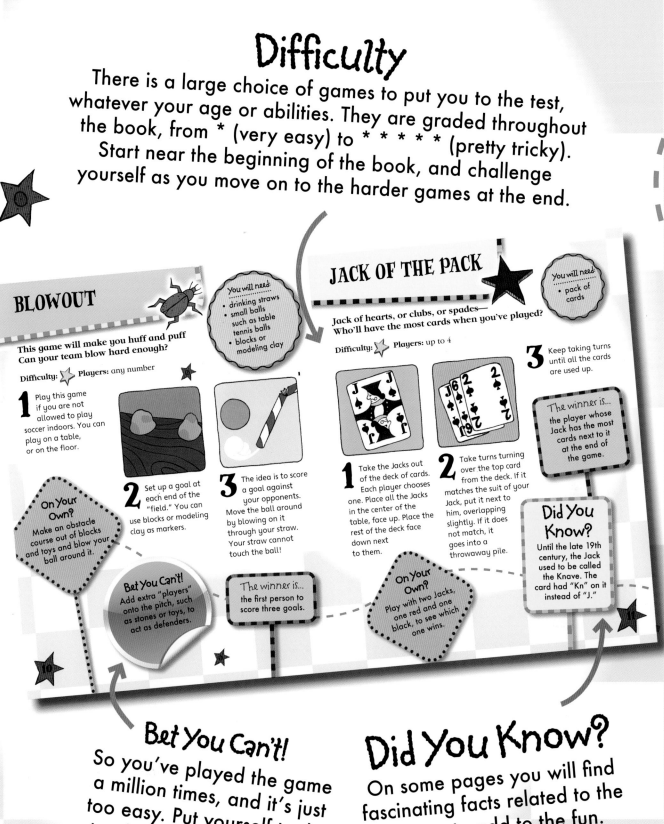

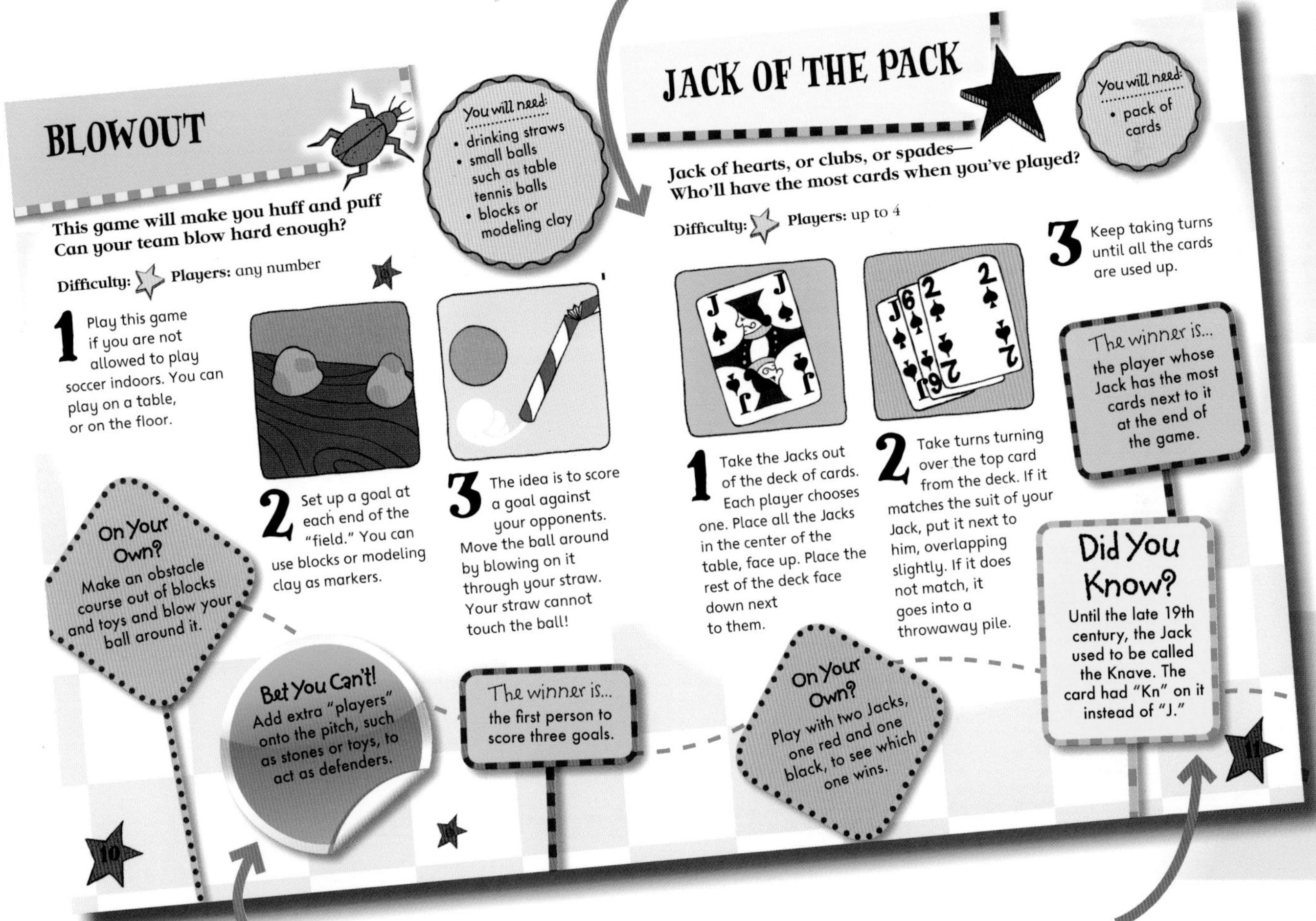

BLOWOUT

This game will make you huff and puff Can your team blow hard enough?

Difficulty: ☆ **Players:** any number

You will need:
- drinking straws
- small balls such as table tennis balls
- blocks or modeling clay

1 Play this game if you are not allowed to play soccer indoors. You can play on a table, or on the floor.

2 Set up a goal at each end of the "field." You can use blocks or modeling clay as markers.

3 The idea is to score a goal against your opponents. Move the ball around by blowing on it through your straw. Your straw cannot touch the ball!

On Your Own? Make an obstacle course out of blocks and toys and blow your ball around it.

Bet You Can't! Add extra "players" onto the pitch, such as stones or toys, to act as defenders.

The winner is... the first person to score three goals.

10

JACK OF THE PACK

Jack of hearts, or clubs, or spades— Who'll have the most cards when you've played?

Difficulty: ☆ **Players:** up to 4

You will need:
- pack of cards

1 Take the Jacks out of the deck of cards. Each player chooses one. Place all the Jacks in the center of the table, face up. Place the rest of the deck face down next to them.

2 Take turns turning over the top card from the deck. If it matches the suit of your Jack, put it next to him, overlapping slightly. If it does not match, it goes into a throwaway pile.

3 Keep taking turns until all the cards are used up.

The winner is... the player whose Jack has the most cards next to it at the end of the game.

Did You Know? Until the late 19th century, the Jack used to be called the Knave. The card had "Kn" on it instead of "J."

On Your Own? Play with two Jacks, one red and one black, to see which one wins.

11

Bet You Can't!

So you've played the game a million times, and it's just too easy. Put yourself to the test by taking the "Bet you can't" challenge, and see how good you are then!

Did You Know?

On some pages you will find fascinating facts related to the games, to add to the fun.

DINOSAUR HUNT

You will need:

- small stuffed animal such as a dinosaur

Hide T. Rex or Brontosaurus,
They'll say, "D'you think he saw us?"

Difficulty: ☆ **Players:** 2 or more

1 One player hides the dinosaur in a room away from the other players.

2 Hide it somewhere tricky to find, but not impossible. It could be on a bookshelf, or by the TV. Don't hide it in the laundry basket—it will never be found!

3 The other players come in and search the room, trying to find the dinosaur.

The winner is... the person who finds the dinosaur—they can hide it next.

On Your Own?

Close your eyes and spin around, then throw the dinosaur. Spin again and open your eyes—and start searching!

Did You Know?

There is an old version of this game called "Hunt the thimble." A thimble is a small, cup-shaped object that fits over a finger—the perfect size for hiding.

WORKS OF ART

You will need:

- scarves
- pencils
- paper

Draw yourself—we think you'll find
It's not so easy drawing blind!

Difficulty: ☆ **Players:** any number

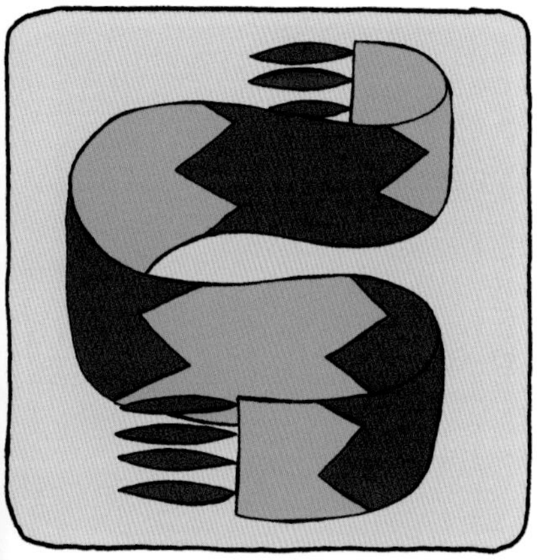

2 Another player names an object for you to draw. It could be your house, yourself or an animal, for instance.

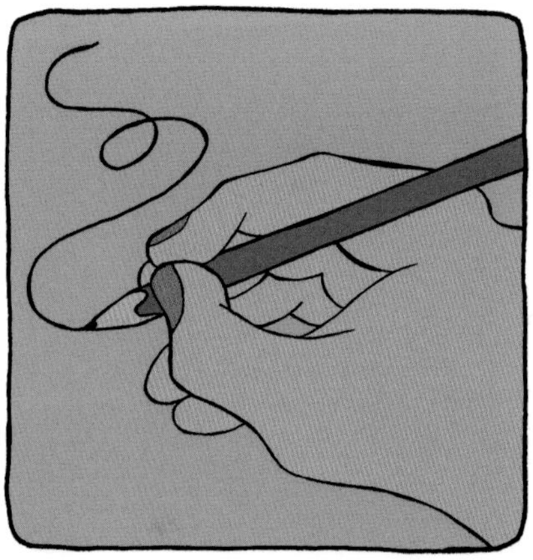

1 Use a scarf as a blindfold—or just close your eyes, but do not cheat!

On Your Own?
Challenge yourself to draw something—no peeking!

3 You must then draw that object without peeking at your paper. When you take a look, you'll laugh at what you've drawn!

The winner is...
no one—this game is just for fun.

Bet You Can't!
Name something the item MUST have, such as the right number of windows on the house.

PENNIES IN THE POT

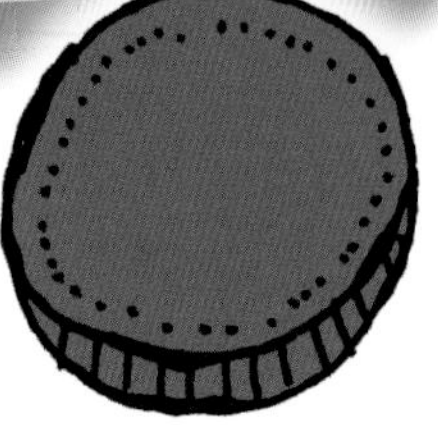

Put your pennies in the pot,
See if you can spend the lot!

Difficulty: ☆ **Players:** 2 or more

You will need:

- 10 counters or coins per player
- 3 dice
- pot or cup

1 Each player chooses a number from one to six. If two people are playing, they choose three numbers each. If there are three players, each one chooses two numbers.

2 Take turns throwing the three dice together. If your number comes up, you can put a counter or a coin in the pot.

3 So, if 1-5-5 is thrown, the player who chose one puts in one coin, and the player who chose five puts in two coins.

The winner is...
the first person to get all their coins in the pot.

On Your Own?

Choose a number and see how many times you have to throw the dice to get all your coins in the pot.

Did You Know?

This game is also called "Help your Neighbor," because you are likely to throw their numbers and help them get rid of their coins.

MATCHING PAIRS

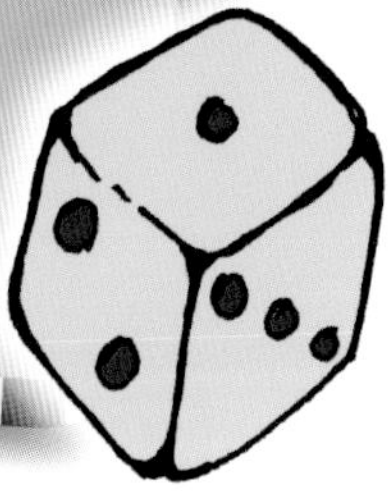

Hide that sock, and hide it well
Or someone might find it by its smell!

Difficulty: ☆ **Players:** 2 or more

You will need:
- pairs of things, such as socks or shoes

1 Gather together lots of pairs of things. Hide one of each pair around the house.

2 Each player is given the other one of a pair, and has to try to find the matching object.

3 It's no use finding a red glove if you're looking for a blue one—you have to find an exact match.

Did You Know?

It could take ages to play this with Joshua Mueller of Washington State—he owns more than 800 pairs of Converse shoes!

On Your Own?

Find things that go together—it could be items such as a bat and a ball, or a spoon and a fork.

The winner is... the first person to find their matching pair.

BLOWOUT

You will need:

- drinking straws
- small balls such as table tennis balls
- blocks or modeling clay

This game will make you huff and puff
Can your team blow hard enough?

Difficulty: ☆ **Players:** any number

1 Play this game if you are not allowed to play soccer indoors. You can play on a table, or on the floor.

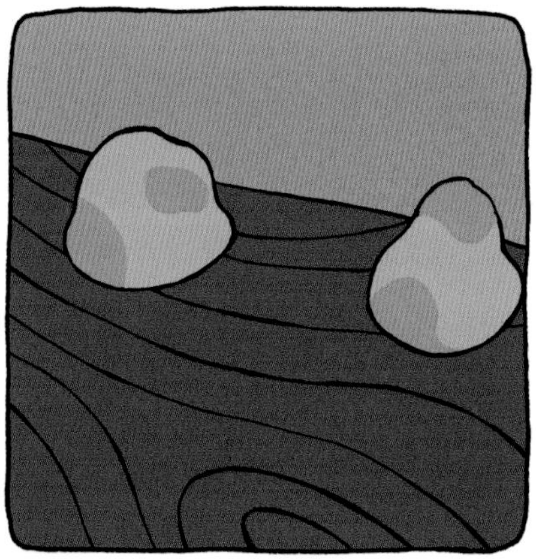

2 Set up a goal at each end of the "field." You can use blocks or modeling clay as markers.

3 The idea is to score a goal against your opponents. Move the ball around by blowing on it through your straw. Your straw cannot touch the ball!

On Your Own?
Make an obstacle course out of blocks and toys and blow your ball around it.

Bet You Can't!
Add extra "players" onto the pitch, such as stones or toys, to act as defenders.

The winner is...
the first person to score three goals.

JACK OF THE PACK

You will need:

- deck of cards

Jack of hearts, or clubs, or spades—
Who'll have the most cards when you've played?

Difficulty: ★ **Players:** up to 4

1 Take the Jacks out of the deck of cards. Each player chooses one. Place all the Jacks in the center of the table, face up. Place the rest of the deck face down next to them.

2 Take turns turning over the top card from the deck. If it matches the suit of your Jack, put it next to him, overlapping slightly. If it does not match, it goes into a throwaway pile.

3 Keep taking turns until all the cards are used up.

The winner is...
the player whose Jack has the most cards next to it at the end of the game.

Did You Know?
Until the late 19th century, the Jack used to be called the Knave. The card had "Kn" on it instead of "J."

On Your Own?
Play with two Jacks, one red and one black, to see which one wins.

DRESSING UP

You will need:

- bags of clothes
- chair

Grab your clothes and put them on! This racing game is fashion fun!

Difficulty: ★ **Players:** 2 equal teams

1 Each team has a bag of clothes. They can be funny beach clothes, like a floppy hat, flip-flops, and a Hawaiian shirt, or any other dress-up outfits. Put them on a chair.

2 Play as a relay race. Player one runs to the chair, puts on all the clothes, runs once around the chair, takes off the clothes and repacks the bag, then runs back to the start.

3 Each player in the team has a turn grabbing the bag and getting dressed and undressed.

The winner is... the first team to finish.

On Your Own?
Beat the clock—can you complete the course in less than two minutes?

Did You Know?
Flip-flops can be seen in wall paintings from ancient Egypt—they were worn by important people.

PICTURE PUZZLE

In your picture what do you see? How many things begin with T?

Difficulty: ☆ **Players:** any number

You will need:

- magazines or travel guides
- pens

2 Each player is given a picture and a letter of the alphabet. Choose common letters such as S, P, or T.

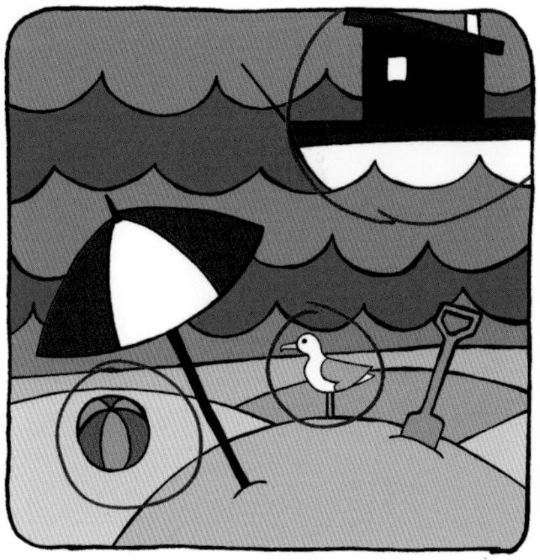

1 Look in magazines for pictures with lots of things going on. Pictures of people at the beach, shopping, or at a theme park are good choices.

On Your Own?

This is a great way to pass some time alone.

3 Draw a circle around all the items in your picture that begin with your letter.

Did You Know?

More English words begin with S or T than with any other letter of the alphabet.

The winner is...

no one, because pictures might just have more things in them than others.

SOCKEY

**Your room is much too small for hockey,
So why not try this game of sockey?**

Difficulty: ☆☆ **Players:** 2 equal teams

You will need:
- long socks
- pieces of candy
- toys
- marbles
- coins

1 Each team has a long sock filled with small items such as toys, wrapped candy, marbles, and coins.

2 One person is the caller and knows what is in each sock. They shout out an item for the teams to bring them.

3 A team can only pull out one item at a time, so if you are trying to find a red marble it's frustrating to keep pulling out a blue one! Score a point if your team hands over the item first.

Bet You Can't!
Fill a sock and see how fast you can find matching pairs, for example two yellow pieces of candy or two pennies.

On Your Own?
Make the game more tricky by putting two large things in the sock that get in the way, such as an apple and a potato.

The winner is...
the team with the most points at the end.

CARD WARS

**Lay your cards out—1, 2, 3, 4,
The winner must get rid of more.**

Difficulty: ★★ **Players:** 2 or more (4 or 5 is best)

You will need:
- deck of cards

1 Deal the cards to the players. It's OK if some players have one more card than others.

2 The player to the left of the dealer puts her lowest card on the table. Let's say it is the 4 of hearts. The player with the 5 of hearts then plays that card, and so on, up to the King of hearts.

3 Whoever played the King then starts the game again, by putting down his lowest card.

The winner is... the first person to get rid of all their cards.

Did You Know?

During the Second World War, playing cards helped US soldiers in prisoner of war camps. Special cards were sent to them containing maps of the area, so they could plan their escape.

On Your Own?

Place the four Aces on the table, then turn the cards over, looking for 2s, then 3s and so on. How many times do you have to work through the deck to complete the four suits?

SINGING STAR

You will need:

- music, from CDs or an MP3 player

Out of tune or singing fine,
See if you can keep in time.

Difficulty: ☆☆ **Players:** any number

1 Take turns choosing a favorite song. Start it playing until it gets to the chorus.

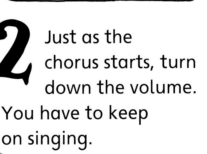

2 Just as the chorus starts, turn down the volume. You have to keep on singing.

3 When you have sung the chorus, turn the music up again. Have you kept in time with the singers?

The winner is...
no one, but some people are much better at this than others.

On Your Own?
No problem—sing all your favorite songs and see how good you are at keeping time.

Bet You Can't!
Turn down the volume during a verse, not the chorus—and try not to forget the words!

TREASURE HUNT

**Ten things to find from drawer and shelf—
Can you collect them by yourself?**

Difficulty: ★★ **Players:** any number

You will need:
- plastic container
- pencils
- paper

1 Each player needs a list of items to find. Use the ideas in step 3, or make up your own. If the players are very young, draw pictures instead.

2 Use your plastic container to collect your items in. It's a race to see who can get all ten items first.

3 Some things to find: teaspoon, coaster, storybook, fruit, paper clip, clothespin, sock, toy car, yellow pen, photograph.

The winner is... the first person to collect all ten things on their list.

On Your Own?

Use the list in step 3 and see how fast you can find everything.

Did You Know?

In the UK, in order for something like buried coins to count as official "treasure" it must be more than 300 years old—so nothing on this list is really treasure!

SARDINES

You will need:

- permission to hide in different rooms

This game's great to play inside,
Find someplace cool where you can hide.

Difficulty: ★★ **Players:** 4 or more

1 One player finds a hiding place, while the other players close their eyes and count to 100.

2 The players split up and try to find the hider. If you find them, join them in their hiding place and keep very quiet.

3 Play keeps going on until the last player finds all the others squeezed in together, under a bed or inside a big closet!

On Your Own?

Draw a map of your house, and mark all the good hiding places with an X.

Did You Know?

This game's name comes from cans of small fish called sardines. Lots of sardines are packed tightly into a small space.

The winner is...
no one, but the last finder becomes the next hider.

SNAP!

Here's a game you'll like to play,
It's perfect for a rainy day.

Difficulty: ☆☆ **Players:** 2

You will need:

- deck of cards

1 Divide the deck in half, so each player has 26 cards. Hold them facing downward, so you can only see the backs.

2 Take turns putting one card each onto a pile in the middle.

3 If you see a card that is the same number or picture as the one before it, shout, "Snap!" If you shout first, you pick up the whole pile. Then keep going as before.

On Your Own?

Play really quickly, turning over cards with both hands. Can you still spot the "Snaps" at top speed?

The winner is...

the person with the most cards, or with the whole deck if you play to the end.

BEETLEDICE

You need to roll a six to start,
Then draw each beetle body part.

You will need:
- pencils
- paper
- dice

Difficulty: ★★ **Players:** 2 or more

1 Take turns throwing the dice, and try to draw a whole beetle. The number you throw tells you which part of the beetle you can draw.

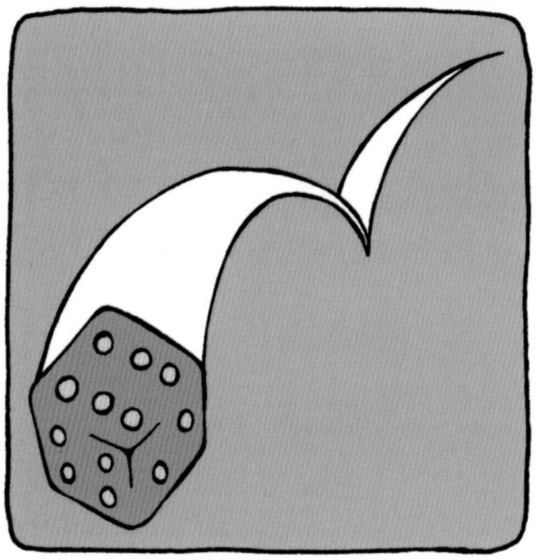

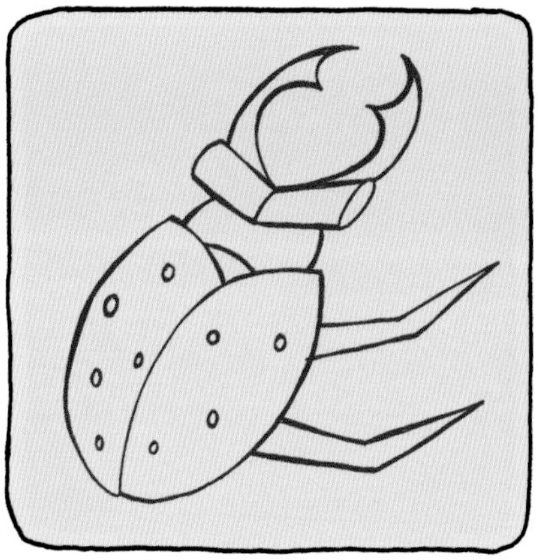

2
6 = body
5 = head
4 = leg
3 = eye
2 = antenna
1 = mouth

3 You can only draw a leg or a head if you have already drawn a body, so you must throw a six first. You may not add eyes, antennae or a mouth until you have drawn the head.

On Your Own?

Draw two different-colored beetles, taking turns throwing the dice for each one, and see which one wins.

Did You Know?

There are more different types of beetle than of any other kind of insect. Maybe your picture is another new species!

The winner is...
the first person to finish drawing a complete beetle, including all six legs.

MOUNTAIN CLIMBING

**Give it your best throw every time—
The number mountain's hard to climb!**

Difficulty: ★★ **Players:** any number

You will need:
- 2 dice
- pencils
- paper

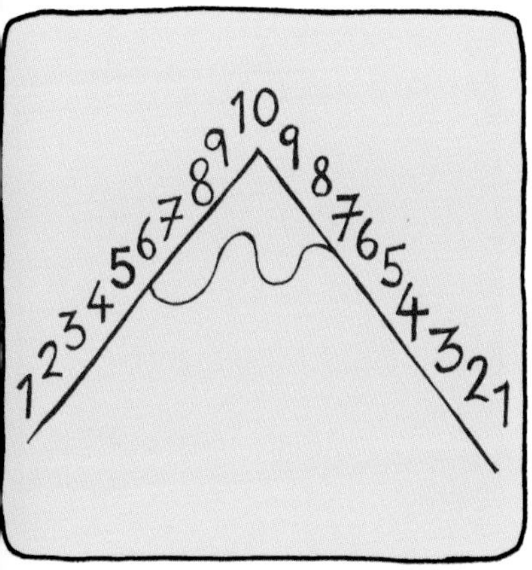

1 Each player writes down the numbers 1 to 10 and back to 1 again, as shown here.

2 Take turns throwing the two dice. Anyone who gets a 1 crosses it off their list. If you are lucky and get a 2 as well, cross that off, too.

3 Keep throwing the dice and crossing off the numbers, in order. To cross out the bigger numbers, add the two numbers on the dice together. For example, if your throw is a 3 and a 4, you can cross off 7 (3 + 4 = 7).

Bet You Can't!

Play with numbers 1 to 12, and cross off the highest ones first.

On Your Own?

See how many turns it takes you to reach the end, and compare your best scores.

The winner is...

the first person to climb their "mountain" of numbers and get back down the other side.

TOTALLY

**Throw high numbers if you're able,
Add the three dice on the table.**

You will need:
- pencils
- paper
- 3 dice

Difficulty: ☆☆ **Players:** 2 or more

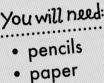

1 The first player throws all three dice. Take out the dice with the highest number, then throw the other two.

2 Take out the dice with the higher number again, then throw the last dice.

3 Get your score by adding up the numbers from all three of your dice. Then let the next player have a turn.

The winner is...
the person with the highest score.

Bet You Can't!

Put a counter in the middle for each player. The winner of each round wins all the counters. If there is a draw, leave the winnings as a "rollover."

On Your Own?

Play in just the same way, trying to beat your own highest score.

ON YOUR MARKS

You will need:
- various items listed in steps 2 and 3

Racing games will keep you busy;
Be careful that you don't get dizzy!

Difficulty: ★★ **Players:** any number

1 You can play racing games indoors as well as outdoors, as long as you play carefully. Use objects that will not break anything. Look at steps 2 and 3 for ideas.

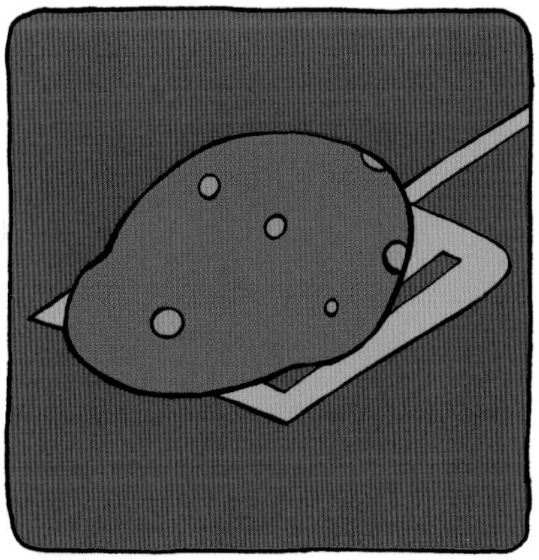

2 Have an egg and spoon race but using a feather in a bowl, or carrying a potato on a spatula. Both are tricky!

3 Give each player a newspaper that they must use to flap a piece of paper across the room. Try crawling along the floor while pushing a ball with your nose, or holding a balloon between your knees.

Bet You Can't!
Wriggle along on your bottom while carrying a marble with your toes.

On Your Own?
Make up your own wacky races, or try to set new solo record times.

The winner is...
the first one to finish, obviously!

RUNNY NOSES

You will need:

- deck of cards
- 2 buckets

Drop a card below your nose,
Fingers crossed for where it goes!

Difficulty: ★★★ **Players:** 2 equal teams

1 Each team stands next to its bucket. Team 1 has the red cards and Team 2 has the black cards.

2 The first player takes a card and holds it so that the short edge touches the bottom of their nose, pointing downward. They let go of the card to see if it falls into the bucket.

3 Player one keeps going, till all of the team's cards are used up. Pick up any tha have missed the bucket, and let player two try with those, and so on.

The winner is...
the first team to get all 26 cards into their bucket.

Did You Know?

Before cards had hearts, diamonds, clubs, and spades, the pictures were coins, cups, swords, and sticks.

On Your Own?

Practice on your own—it's harder than it sounds!

DICE GOLF

**It's hard to score a hole in one,
But trying can be lots of fun.**

You will need:

- pencils
- paper
- 3 dice

Difficulty: ★★★ **Players:** any number

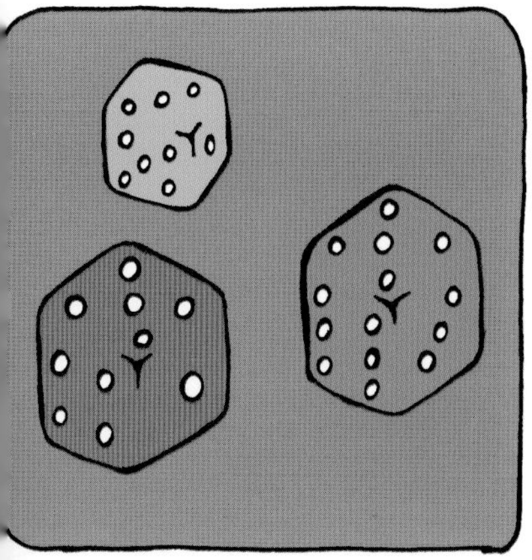

1 On your turn, throw the three dice together. You are trying to get a double—for example, two fives.

2 If you don't get two of the same number, try again. Keep track of how many throws it takes to score your double. That's one 'hole' finished.

3 Let each player take a turn at throwing. Everyone needs to get 18 doubles, like the 18 holes of a golf course. Keep track of all the scores.

The winner is...
the person with the lowest score after 18 holes.

On Your Own?
Play in the same way, and keep a record of your best scores.

Bet You Can't!
Score a hole in one—a double on your first throw!

PEA BRAINS

Suck really hard to move those peas,
Try not to spill them, if you please!

Difficulty: ☆☆☆ **Players:** any number

You will need:

- 10 peas per player
- small bowls
- straws

1 Each player needs an empty bowl and a drinking straw. Place a bowl of peas (or chocolate chips—even better!) between the players.

2 Each player tries to suck a pea onto the end of their straw, then move it across to their own bowl. Everyone plays at once.

3 Stop when all the peas have been sucked up. Ignore any that have fallen on the floor—yuck!

The winner is... the player with the most peas in their bowl.

Did You Know?

A company in Seattle, Washington, has made a green-pea-flavored soda. Now that would be easy to suck up with your straw!

On Your Own?

See how many peas you can move in one minute.

BASKETBALL

You will need:
- soft ball
- wastebasket

Who can throw their ball the best? This game will put you to the test.

Difficulty: ☆☆☆ **Players:** any number

1 Place a wastebasket on one side of the room. Take four steps backwards.

2 The idea is to score a "basket" by throwing or bouncing the ball into the wastebasket.

3 You are allowed three tries. If you miss, you are out. If you are successful, you go through to the next round, where you have to take an extra step backwards.

The winner is...
the person who qualifies for the most rounds.

Did You Know?

When real basketball was invented, they used peach-collecting baskets—so this game is pretty similar!

On Your Own?

Practice makes perfect! It's fun playing this alone.

CARD LOTTERY

You will need:
- deck of cards

"Higher! Lower!" you must shout,
But two the same will catch you out!

Difficulty: ★★★ **Players:** any number

1 Shuffle the cards, then turn over the top one.

2 Player one has to say if the next card is going to be higher or lower than the one showing. That's easy if it's a King, but harder if it's a middle card like a 7.

3 Player one keeps going until they get one wrong. (If the next card is the same number, you are also out.) The turned-over cards are theirs to keep. The next player now has a turn.

The winner is... the person holding the most cards after three turns each.

Did You Know?
This game used to be a TV game show called Card Sharks.

On Your Own?
You can still play, guessing "higher" or "lower" before you turn over each card.

WHERE IN THE WORLD?

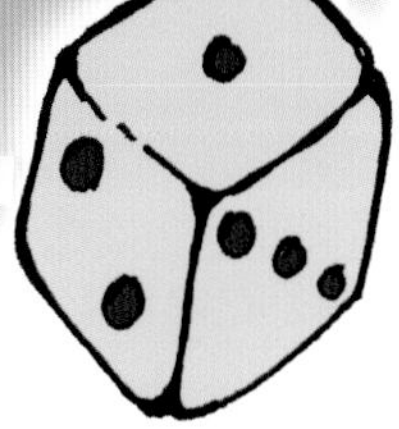

Rack your brains for all you're worth
To work your way around the Earth.

Difficulty: ☆☆☆☆ **Players:** any number

You will need:
- map of the world
- pencil

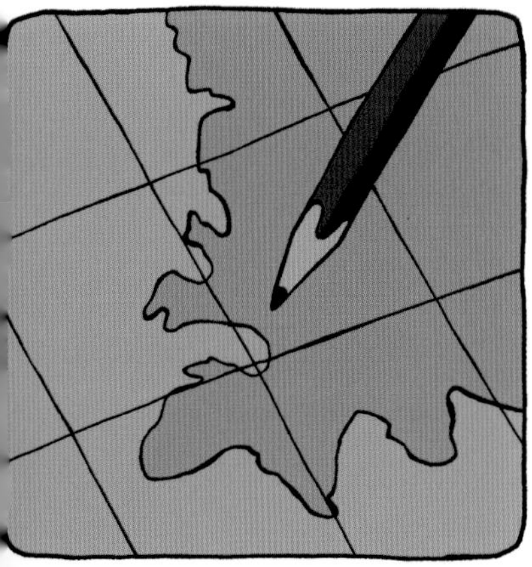

Open up the map and take turns closing your eyes and pointing to a place with the pencil.

2 Each player scores a point for knowing about their chosen country: which continent it is on, its capital city and the main language spoken. Use the map or an atlas or an encyclopedia to check the answers.

3 Score extra points for additional facts, such as currency, famous places, or famous people from your country.

The winner is...

everyone—it's better to play just for fun, because it's easier to answer questions about some countries than others.

On Your Own?

This is still fun—pick places at random and test your own knowledge.

Did You Know?

The biggest country in the world is Russia, but the country with the most people is China.

HIDE AND SNAP

You will need:

- 2 decks of cards

Memory's good and eyes are keen?
Try to remember what you've seen.

Difficulty: ☆☆☆☆ **Players:** 2 equal teams

1 Before you play, someone hides the cards from one deck, individually, around the house. You could hide them in bookshelves, or in the fridge, or under furniture.

2 This player then hands out cards from the other deck to all team members. They have to find the matching card and return it to the "hider" to score a point. They are then given another card to match.

3 Compare cards with your teammates and help each other search.

The winner is... the team with the most points after a set time.

Bet You Can't!
Remember which cards you have seen, so you can find the pairs more quickly.

On Your Own?
Hide the cards yourself, face down, then play the game to match them all up.

JACKS

Pick up jacks and catch the ball:
See if you can scoop them all.

Difficulty: ☆☆☆☆ **Players:** any number

You will need:

- set of jacks or some pebbles
- small bouncy ball

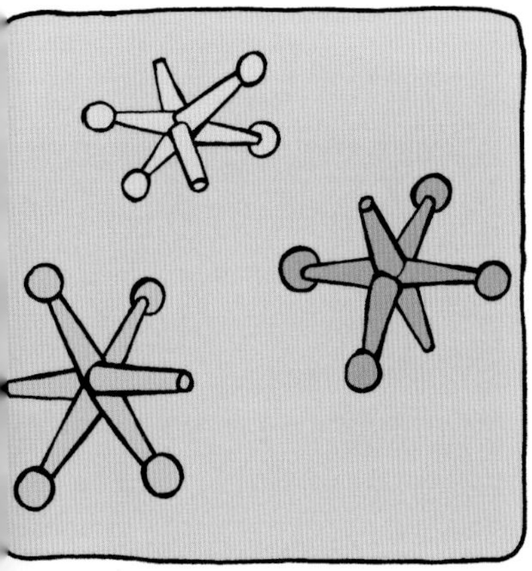

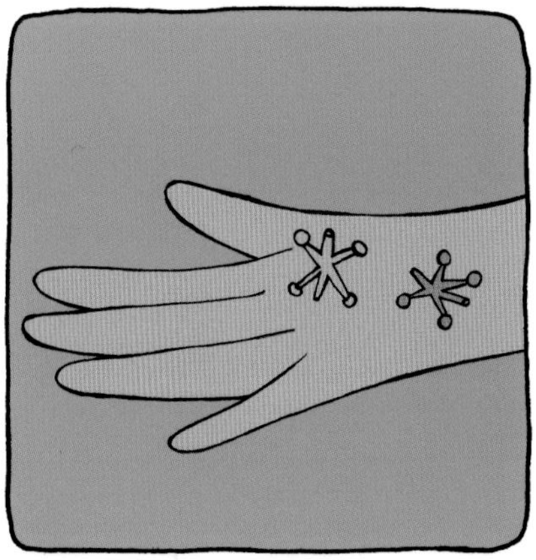

1 Set out your jacks or pebbles in a row. It is easiest to play on a hard floor or a table.

2 Bounce your ball gently, and while it is in the air, scoop up one jack. Use the hand holding the jack to catch the ball after it bounces a second time.

3 Now do it again scooping up two jacks, then three, then four...

The winner is... the person who can scoop up the most jacks and still catch the ball.

On Your Own? No problem—this game was designed to play alone.

Bet You Can't! Catch the ball before it bounces a second time!

COIN CATCHER

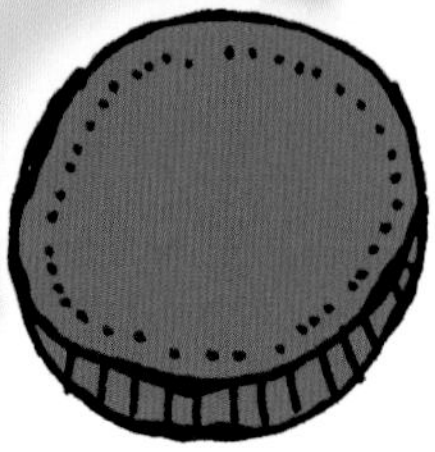

You will need:

- about 10 coins of the same value

Pile the coins and flip them all,
Then catch them quick: don't let them fall!

Difficulty: ☆☆☆☆☆ **Players:** any number

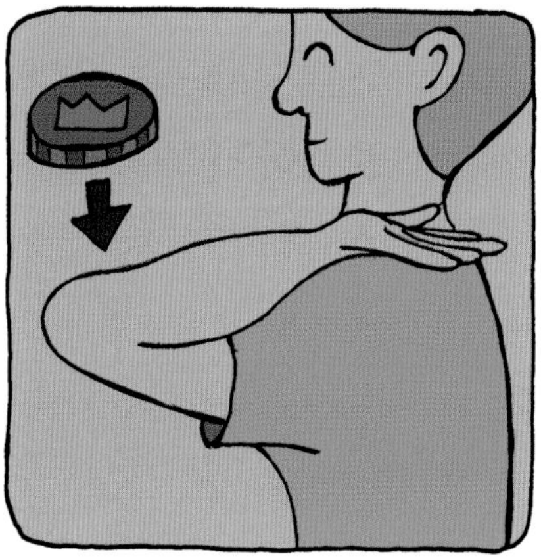

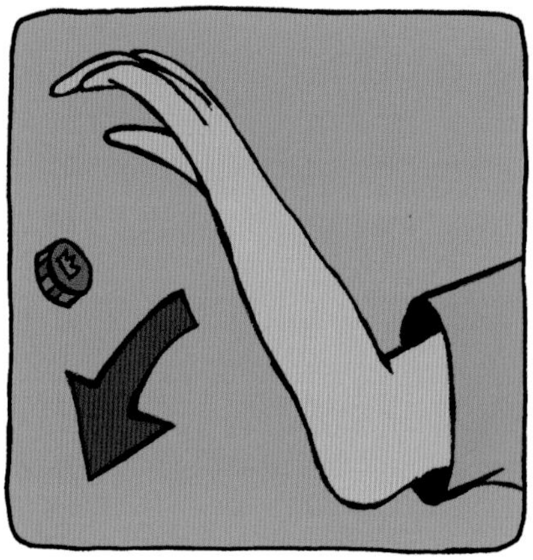

1 Bend your arm back so that your hand rests on top of your shoulder, as in the picture.

2 Place a coin on the flat part of your elbow. Now flip your arm down so the coin flies off—can you catch it in mid-air with the hand of that arm?

3 When you can catch one coin, try again with two or more coins in a pile.

The winner is... the person who can catch the biggest tower of coins.

Bet You Can't!
Catch more than ten coins in a pile!

On Your Own?
This game is perfect to play alone, and later you show off your skill to your friends.